MIDDAY SHADOWS

Midday Shadows

by

Armando P. Ibañez

VANTAGE PRESS
New York / Washington / Atlanta
Los Angeles / Chicago

FIRST EDITION

All rights reserved, including the right of
reproduction in whole or in part in any form.

Copyright © 1980 by Armando P. Ibañez

Published by Vantage Press, Inc.
516 West 34th Street, New York, New York 10001

Manufactured in the United States of America
Standard Book Number 533-04028-0

Library of Congress Catalog Card No.: 78-64689

ACKNOWLEDGMENTS

The Canto Al Pueblo National Board published "The Vigil" in *An Anthology of Experiences*, June 1978.

Gráficia Magazine published "A Walking Man," "La Lechusa," and "¿Qué Señora?" in its May-June 1976 issue.

A todas y a todos mis camaradas, Gracias.

DEDICATION

A El y mis padres Geronimo y Vicenta

INTRODUCTION

The reader will find in this book three kinds of poems. These are: those that are written in Spanish; those that are written in English; and still those that are written by combining both English and Spanish. The reader may immediately ask why the author writes in such a style, especially the latter.

The answer to such a question is very simple. The reason is that the author can think in both *English* and *Spanish*. As a matter of fact, many Chicanos can think, and consequently speak, in this manner. Many term this communication style as "Tex-Mex."

Language is communication. And "Tex-Mex" fits this description. Therefore, why not reflect this verbal communication in written form? Thus, I decided years ago to write in this style—that which is very dear to me—poetry.

The next question the reader may ask is: "What is poetry?" The answer depends on the individual, as interpretation of literature also depends on the individual. Poetry is an art. Thus, such a question is synonymous to that which asks, "What is art?" Poetry, an art, is an expression of the inner being of man. It is a form of communication between the soul of man and God, man and nature, man and abstract, man and man.

In communicating, a poem takes the form of being an entity in itself. It lives. This is the reason poems, like great art, survive the trials of time many years after their human creators have left this world. They have become living testimonies in their own right. This is why a poem does not necessarily convey only what its author intended or may not have intended. A poem, like a painting or a song, is there for man to feel. It is there, ready to comfort, arouse or inspire the inner being of man depending on the interpretation. For example, a chair is an object. But as an object, it may represent comfort for a nonparalytic while it may represent challenge to a paralytic. It is still a chair. The object has not changed; only how it is perceived has changed. The same holds true in poetry.

Poetry is poetry, as art is art. Great poems have been written in many languages. The language of a poem does not restrict it from acquiring its rightful place. After all, poetry is an expression of the soul of man and language is a tool of this expression. Consequently, why not write in "Tex-Mex"—which is a form of communication?

CONTENTS

Book One—Poems

Part I

The Black Cloud 3
El Sapo 4
The Rolling Barrel* 5
Nacer* 7
Mi Angel 7
Droplets* 8
Cosas of the World* 9
Rayos of the Sun* 12
Chulo y Lepe 14
Sunlight 15
La Lechusa* 15
Coracol 17
Yo* 17
Belinda 18
Eyes 19
Earth 19
Napkins 20
Things to Do 20
Grito* 21
El Viejito 21
On a Binge 24

Part II

Face 26
Las Nubes* 27
He 28

* English translations in Book Two—Translations

Buttercups 28
A Passing Light 29
The Leaf 30
Gusanito* 31
¿Qué Señora?* 32
Luela* 33
The Vigil 34
A Poner* 35
The Forest* 36
A Sembrar* 37
Roses* 38
Mi Señora* 39
¿Tú? 40
Powerless 40
La Luz del Diá 41
A Sparrow on a Walk 41
Mestizos* 42
Soy 42

Part III

Death 43
Highway 44 44
Contemplating 45
A Sprouting Bean 45
El Piscador* 46
No Name* 47
Chella* 48
The Ceiling 49
La Lamparita Sin Luz* 49
Esperanza* 50
Just a Tree 51
To Visualize* 52
Who? 53
Un Hombre* 54
Viendo al Cielo* 55
Una Mujer* 56

Los Sueños* 58
Just Wondering 63
Arroyo 63
Paper 64
Esperando* 64

Part IV

Dreaming 65
Macario* 66
Reflections 68
A Flying Thing 69
Aqui y Aya 70
Sombra* 71
Sometimes a Proud Star 71
Enticement 72
A Meduza 73
Un Niño 74
Sitting Alone* 75
A Walking Man* 77
Mezquite Tree 78
This Building* 79
Unos Ojos* 80
Midnight Sun 81
¿Ella Es?* 81
¿Tú Eres?* 82
An Intoxicated Moon 83
Mi Surco* 83
Writing Can Be 84

Book Two—Translations

The Rolling Barrel 87
Nacer 88
Droplets 89
Cosas of the World 90
Rayos of the Sun 92

La Lechusa 94
Yo 95
Grito 96
Las Nubes 96
Gusanito 97
¿Qué Señora? 98
A Poner 99
The Forest 100
A Sembrar 101
Roses 102
Mi Señora 103
Mestizos 104
El Piscador 104
No Name 105
Chella 106
La Lamparita Sin Luz 107
Esperanza 108
To Visualize 109
Un Hombre 110
Viendo al Cielo 111
Una Mujer 112
Los Sueños 114
Esperando 118
Macario 119
Sombra 120
Sitting Alone 121
A Walking Man 123
This Building 124
Unos Ojos 125
¿Ella Es? 126
¿Tú Eres? 127
Mi Surco 128

MIDDAY SHADOWS

BOOK ONE

PART I

Opening our eyes, we eventually see the light.

THE BLACK CLOUD

The ears of the black cloud
dragged on the hairline of the earth.
she rumbled.
throwing her flashes of light
she growled at the world below.
the sweet smell of a freshly-bathed soil
penetrated the cotton fields
as rattlesnakes slid off their skins
beneath the cactus plants.

She threw more light.
 with clenched fists she pounced the earth,
rumbled, screamed and howled at everything that moved
till exhausted she fell to silence.
the empathetic sun cuddled and comforted her to sleep.

EL SAPO

    There you lie,
    victim of oppression,
        with guts and brains
        exposed to the cold air
    as thousands of insect hands
quickly inspect your corpse
to see what can be salvaged.

    Yesterdays.
    do you remember the day
      when you were carefree,
          free to the world?
    the days that rained,
        the glorious ones,
      when you hopped
      and sang your song
          which no one listened
          to its beauty . . . but
          you didn't care . . . ˙as you sang even more.

Yes,
   you were *you*,
      you poor ugly thing
        and because of *you*
           you lie here dead.

THE ROLLING BARREL

Un barril lleno de aire
empezo to roll down *la bajadita del arroyo*.
slowly . . . slowly . . . it rolled . . .
gathering speed as it went . . .
faster . . . faster . . . faster it ran
kissing *las piedras de caliche*
and waving, "bye" to *los quelites*
and shouting, "look at me, i'am free!"

it glided gracefully
as it splashed
in the muddy water *del arroyo*.
there it enthusiastically swayed *de lado a lado*
bathing itself as it floated down the creek
till somewhat tired it came to a halt
on the banks of this majestic place.
it ran no further.

Some tiny growing hands
baked by *los rayos de la luna y el sol*
picked it up again.
su panza llena de agua
gritaba de gusto
as it again began to roll down the same *bajadita*
as before.
now at even a faster pace
it flew down.
no podia besar las piedras
because of its great speed.

los quelites y los mezquites
se abrazaban unos a los otros
y carcajeandose y burlandose
en la tierra se arrastraban.

Jumping and bouncing
it rolled down ever-so-fast.
desperately it tried to grab
los manos de las nubes
that watched it without concern.

Till finally,
el grito de la llorona
stabbed every creature to silence
as *la boca del arroyo* slowly *se lo trago.*
down in the very depths of the creek
it is buried
never to be seen again.

NACER

*¿Por qué me sigue
esta sombra de nada?
la sombra de hacer
pero siempre vivir en sueños
sueños de nacer.*

MI ANGEL

An angel lazily floated in the sky.
his grey veil
moist with rain drops
gently fell on the thirsty grass below.

He scratched his head
and playfully tossed his silver gray hair
that captivated the sun's smile.
while teasing the trees
with his cool breath
he knelt on the hill to pray to the heavens.

Spreading his wings
he kissed the earth
and gracefully flew towards the west
where he met the others
and quietly left.

DROPLETS

Las lagrimas de almas lloronas
are flowing
        in the body of earth
in lakes,
    rivers
        and fall as droplets
        of diamonds
to awaiting hands.

The eyes and lips
of the king of apes
give a sparkle and speak of terms.
a sparkling light
        that has glimmered
since the birth of time
set to invite,
    as guests,
        its prey.
then to become knives and swords
with a coat of blood and torn flesh.
y sueltan los gritos
        de aires en batalla.

the crowned king
of colored lights,
        plastics and jets
gives his words
of promises and love.

lips of firmness
                and tenderness
assure the spoken words
with laws from heaven.
yet the sharp teeth
                sink into warm flesh
making the blood spurt
                and smear his face.
y sueltan los gritos
de aires en batalla.

Las lagrimas de almas lloronas
are flowing in the body of earth
in lakes, rivers and falls as droplets
                of diamonds.

COSAS OF THE WORLD

Salen del humano unas manos
showing the traces of their veins
rascan
    la tierra
making holes
that fill with *un vomito*
    y la pobre tierra
    responde
        with shrieking sounds
        de almas perdidas
piercing the heart of silence.

A menace
este llorido
    ensucia las sabanas
    of the human race
it turns the golden thrones and crowns
    to a mossy green
    cosas podridas.

Y el grito sigue
    it follows the wind
    falls with the rain
las ramas
de cada cosa
    detienen
    the captive souls.

The chieftains
of every tribe
    comienzan su baile
    they fan the spirits
    with their golden feathers
their chanting voices
and their splashing feet
    smear *la gente*
    bañense!
    tomen parte!

Se hacen playas del vomito
aqui se baña la gente
    llena de alegria
    con risas y carcajadas
the nails of the gnawing hands
    become red
    with filth
y la gente sigue
    with their games
    and laughter
only
    the groaning sounds
    of struggling winds
    se oyen
    en unos oidos.

RAYOS OF THE SUN

Los rayos del sol
acompañados con el aire
brush every blade of grass
that stands or bows.
la gente con muchas caras
    se rie y anda por el mundo
making codes and proclamations
    thanking God for life.
las nubes en el cielo
sueltan su llorido
    on every plant and person.
a furious wind *sumba*
entre los arboles
shouting in the ears of every person:
    "*¡Mirame! ¡Pon cuidado!*"

Encircled with lights
of every conceivable color
people watch to see
    their mold take form,
impuesta a su lado.

From the dirt
    a mumbled shriek
filters through the surface
muy cansado
aguantando los pisones de la fiesta.

no one listens
only laughter rumbles
so very hard *que tiemblan*
    las montañas y las olas del mar.
the birds and the flowers
    vuelta y vuelta cain.
lightning, *de venganza,*
red with fire
  apunta a toda cosa
to suck the blood
   of every walking creature.

Se apagan las luces
del humano.
   they're running in darkness
   otros arrastrandose gritan:
      "¡Yo! ¡Yo!"
Everything pukes
   el exceso del agua
until nothing stands
nomas el vomito
   color de todo muerto

Calmness returns
    to the skies.
y el mundo
mirandose muy quieto
empieza a resoyar.
from the dirt
  come
  the frogs
  el nuevo Rey.

CHULO Y LEPE

Chulo, a purple cat
and *Lepe*, a green polka-dotted dog,
wrestled playfully
on the banks of *el arroyo*.

Chulo with his eyes of gold
gently bit *Lepe* on his ear.
the *arroyo* smiled
as he enjoyed seeing his children
play this way.

The giant plaided pecan tree
hollered to *Chulo*,
"Hey climb on me!
and you'll see all there is to see."
without giving it a second thought
the carefree cat jumped on the tree.
there he could see,
as the tree had promised,
everything!

Colorful stars floated from his mouth
as he said, "*Lepe* . . . come see!"
the green polka-dotted dog
could not join the cat
'cause he had grown sails
and floated to the sun.

SUNLIGHT

Yawning
the sun awoke
it stretched
its arms
and gently tickled
the moon.

She gave him
a smile
turned on her side
and went to sleep.

LA LECHUSA

En una noche limpia de nubes
i sat on my front porch
a esperar lo que fuera de la noche.

I remember it so well
porque lo que les voy a platicar
es algo duro para comprender
pero cierto.

Volando cerca de la luna
gritaba la lechusa blanca
que mucha gente dice que es bruja.
gritaba cosas that my ears
couldn't comprehend
pero mi alma se temblaba de frio.

la cara de la luna
se puso anaranjada
de vergüenza.
que cosas serian
that this creature
spouted to me . . . or to the earth?

I reached high to the sky
and grabbed that moon's passing light
and held it close to my chest
hoping *que esa cosa*
se pasara y no volviera.

The cool hands of the wind
slapped me back . . . it's just an owl.
 . . . nothing to worry about . . .
it's not logical.
feeling more at ease i petted *mi perrita*
that sat right beside me.
i grabbed her
flapped my wings
and flew towards *la luna* to turn in for the night.

CORACOL

In its shell
it lives
moving slowly
at times even slower.

Its black wires
it uses as its hands
moving about
feeling every stone.

Back to its shell
it goes
waiting to move again.

YO

Soy el mascarado
that penetrates
every feeling *y todo pulso.*
miro todo con un ojo grande y verde.
i am in every man *esperando a salir.*
i board every ship, *carro y tren.*

Sí, i've traveled through
the canals of time and space.
estoy aqui y estoy aya
waiting to show myself
and proclaim my very being!

Pero no se puede
'cause you might . . . harm me . . . or kill me.
¿matar me?
¡imposible! si nunca muero.

BELINDA

So today is your birthday.
you say you're eighteen,
graduating from high school!
a big girl you say you are,
i mean a woman.
excuse me it's just that i forget
how fast time can pass.

You, your dad, your mom and everyone
has grown in many ways while
taking things in stride.
but at times it seemed hopeless to go on.
"life" you've heard it said
has its "ups and downs."
overused is the phrase
but how true is what it says.

Belinda, lecture you i will not try
i only want to say what is on these lines.
be careful, Binda,
take it slow.
and when you think you don't know
just stop, rest, and it'll come to you
as easily as the air you breathe.

EYES

Eyes
     eyes
          everywhere
they don't blink
they only stare
hung on every wall
        of closed corridors
            and endless halls.

EARTH

The bright
glittering eyes
of flying eagles
in the night
smile at the face
of earth.

She vested
in a gown
dripping with tears
that stream
to almost every part
of her
stares at the vast universe
and returns their gentle smile.

NAPKINS

Words on paper napkins
will only soak
the spillings of the drink
it holds.

But there
through the night
it lives in its world
till the morning comes
and claims its hold.

THINGS TO DO

I am a builder of things
that need neither brick, stone nor wood
but loose grains of sand.
i create dunes on every beach
and sand castles near the waves.

My work is never finished
as sand constantly falls
from my jet-black hair.
yes, i am a builder with endless work
till the time comes to die.

GRITO

Cuando oyi un grito
run through *las ramas
de los* trees,
la luna desperto.

*¿Los perros ladraban
o cantaban?
no recuerdo . . . yo.*

EL VIEJITO

An old man
sat on his butt
playing with his crutches.
he fondled his right thigh
searching for his leg
which he knew was gone.
some say he lost it
en las piscas
when he attempted
to kill a rattlesnake.

The hot wind
freely ran its fingers
through the porch
where this old man sat.
he thought of times
when his arms didn't complain
of rheumatism or arthritis.

he smiled when he thought
of the days when his fingers
easily caressed a woman's hair
and played with her nipples.

A stray dog crossed
the highway from where he sat,
and ran towards
the tall dry buffalo grass.
the old man stared at its tail
till emptiness caressed it to nothing.
his nostrils suddenly awoke
to the smell of moist grass
and his eyes could clearly see
the buck that got away
nearly thirty-five years ago.

He stroked his long white beard
and unbuttoned his red shirt
as the wind whispered in his ear
hot and humid words.
the drops of sweat
rolled from his forehead
just as heavily as they did when
he rode "Chino," his horse,
quite some time ago.

Chino was no thoroughbred
but in being just a horse
he was of a special breed.
he plowed *los acres*,
pulled heavy loads and
ran in countless races
where some were won and some were lost.
The old man's dark eyes
attempted to focus on the shadow
that ran past him.

los años se han pasado
many yesterdays of accomplishments
and of broken promises have lapsed.
dreams that waited to be born
have become old and stale
never to breathe.

Reaching for his hip-pocket
he sighed
and brought out his notes
on the novel he had been working
since he was a boy
the novel that was going
to make him world famous
was only a scribbled thought.
his notes now seemed strange.
they had become animals
holding time prisoner
within their claws
a dead fetus.
stale and dry.

He grabbed his crutches
swung them to his side
and got up.
walking towards the mesquite tree
he sought out the shadow.
he looked and walked.
walked and looked.
he was fearful of it
but he had to see it
for reasons unknown to him.
he finally threw his crutches
and got it by its throat
till he and the shadow died.

ON A BINGE

Sitting at the edge of a bar
i sipped my drink,
rattled my glass
and sighed as the gulp of liquor
slid down my insides.

I remember i started slow
but sooner than i thought
i lost count of my "just a few."
i spoke to strangers
and said many things that i never
thought i could say.
i was king,
knew it all.
i was one of the attractive ones there.

Joyce, the girl from the office,
walked in the joint.
i bought her a bourbon and coke.
after many a sip and gulp
we exhausted the night with our eloquent steps
of dances that i didn't know i knew.

Locked with each other our bodies kept pace.
we kissed and petted
in full view of the thousand watchful eyes
that did the same or at least entertained
such thoughts of doing so.

oh, what a night!
it was too good to come to an end.

i took her to my room
where we continued our partying.
we drank some more,
danced with the walls
and our eyes fell to the floor.

Her dark eyes said, "come lay with me."
an invitation i could not refuse,
i undid her blouse.
while caressing her bare breasts
i conked out, dead drunk, in bed.

PART II

We walk unknown paths and never see the trees.

FACE

A mystic face
embraced with blood and pus
pierces through the curtain of the night.
its smile with green slime
filters through the fingers of time
to lure an unknowing soul
many of which fly through the universe
and swim the cool waters.

A carefree soul it is
that plays with the moon and earth
who bathe him with their gown of wanting
and their arms caress his breast.

Unknowingly he follows the lure
to the forsaken place
where the red glittering eyes of the mystic face
capture his being.

LAS NUBES

*Me acoste
en mi costal de algodon.
viendo al cielo
las nubes levantaron
sus faldas
y empezaron a correr.*

*Yo les gritaba
que se desvolvieran
para darles un apreton
y que regaran mi corazon.*

*Haciendome este favor
sintiera mi alma
fresca y libre
de este gato prieto
que duerme en mi pasion.*

HE

His cool breath
moves the castles
of creamy white
and gray
to a special place.

His golden eye
shines with brilliance
on silver spoons
and knives.

Till this very day
i await to die.

BUTTERCUPS

Pink buttercups with yellow mouths
sang and danced to the music of the wind.
their hands high in the air
swayed to the mystical beat.

Their neighbor, the carpet grass,
growled with annoyance,
"stop the singing and that silly dancing!
or i'll choke you to death!"

Paying no attention
the dancing buttercups
took off their skirts
and danced naked with the wind.

A PASSING LIGHT

A passing light
penetrated his being
blinding his eyes.
he fluttered them
trying to focus
but only blotches
of multicolored ink
appeared on the screen.

Oh!
what a light!
exploding in his inners
rushing to his heart
       his mind
            his soul!
oh yes!
he's electrified!

What man is this
running through the brush
as vicious cactus plants
lower their shields
and fire their spears?

He runs
   flies
      jumps high
          high, high,
              high to the sky
while the cool breath
of the moon
soothes his wild heart.

Slowly,
slowly,
    gently he floats down
        down to the bosom of the earth
to nurse again
only feeling
    a warm sensation
    of ashes past.

THE LEAF

A flowing leaf
from a restless wind
without any ties
    or any kin
        dances
        on this crazy place.

Merrily it sings
whirling
and twirling
    to an audience
        that's deaf
        but not mute.

Soon it'll be dust
    flying in the wind.

GUSANITO

Que gusto me da
ver la paloma
volar del sol.

Fluttering its wings
descansa en su nido
para empezar su cancion.

Sale el gusano,
squirming out of its hole
pegandose en el pecho
da su grito, "vete al sol!"

Al llegar el gato prieto
la palomita termina su cancion.
se va siguiendo la sombra del sol.

Y el gusanito se mete
en su poso
a comer su frijol.

¿QUÉ SEÑORA?

*En una mañana serenosa
una viejita vestida de negro
andaba por las calles de San Diego.
su cabello color de harina
bailaba en el aire.
los perros ladraban
y los gatos se escondian.*

*Llegando al la esquina
de la calle mier y la carretera 44
se paro.
despues,
que sus ojos de pasa
inspectaron la region,
se sento.*

*Abriendo su bolsio azul
saco una carta,
amarilla de años.
y los mezquites empezaron a gritar.
los gatos salieron de donde estaban
a platicar con ella
que leia su carta con mucha atencion.*

*La agilia morada
volaba cerca
buscando su sombra.*

al ver la señora anciana
un ataque le dio.
cayo del cielo y murio.

Levantandose se limpio sus manos.
anduvo donde el cuerpo del pajaro cayo.
con mucho cuidado hecho
la agilia y carta a su bolsio.
al llorar el sol
ella se desaparecio.

LUELA

The glaring fingers
of an apathetic light
punctured Luela's green nostrils.
It didn't bother her much
as she breathed in
my expelled breath.

Oh, Luela
How beautiful you are!
Luela, my rubber plant.

THE VIGIL

The moon peeked
through the strands
of hair
that clung
loosely to the sun.
she brushed 'em aside
and covered the land
with her blue veil.

Silently
her brothers and sisters
joined her
on the watch
a vigil perhaps.

A blue racer
roared through
the streets
chasing its shadow
as the cat sat
on its haunches
watching,
waiting.

The moon smiled,
petted the cat,
and walked away.

A PONER

Un gallito viejo
con plumas coloradas
controlaba su gallinero.
Siempre se acostaba
con las mejores gallinas.

No le importaba,
si eran prietas, blancas
colaradas o pintas.
quealcabo todas
huevos ponen.

THE FOREST

From the fertile earth
a human plant emerges
with its arms clasped
together pointing towards the sky
se estienden
a carisiar los rayos del sol,
manos morenas
that played with the wind
swaying *de lado a lado.*

The barren fields become forests
as they multiply
bailando con la luz de la luna
y las estrellas.

Blooms of murky white
decorate the blue walls
of the heavens
as *las rayas coloradas*
run through their fields
catching every seed
making them sterile.
They live
and breathe
porque sus años estan contados
when they'll return
to the earth,
and be no more!

A SEMBRAR

Piscando las palabras
de mi pasado
me senté en mi surco
a contarlas.

Un libro
of these words and phrases
i was to make
rogando que alas les salieran
so that they would
fly through *las lavores*
and in time
become a new breed
en la siembra de algodon.

ROSES

El rosal se puso su traje verde
a esperar que viniera el hombre,
el hombre que le daba
sus joyas hechas de rubis.

Sus ojos brillaban de llanto
y desesperacion.
"¿hay . . . cuando viene mi hombre?"
le preguntaba a la colmena
que volaba cerca.
"no se, mujer . . . pero ojala que sea pronto
porque yo tambien . . . espero a ver tus joyas.
se que son lujosas . . . y por eso voy atocarlas
para que no se pierdan causa de un mal de ojo."

Al llegar el hombre
grito el vecino del rosal
que era un arbol,
"miren todos! ya llego el hombre!
miren que el rosal ya trai sus joyas!
joyas brillantes!"
"mira . . . que curioso" dijo la colmena,
"no son rubis pero oro."
Y el rosal nomas un suspiro dio.

MI SEÑORA

Mi señora es una mujer
vestida con un deseo para servir
sus hijos, nietos y primos.
con sus manos morenas
ella los baña y los peina.

Recuerdo,
que en el veinte y cuatro de diciembre
ella dio su regalo humano
a sus parientes
gustosos unos de ellos
se bañaron en el rio de nada
pero lleno de las estrellas, luna y sol.

Ahora,
dicen que mi señora
va y besa a su gente
y les dice, "abrazen a la lumbre del sol
porque viene mi hijo, el Rey."

¿TÚ?

There you are!
dancing on
the veil
of emptiness
as glittering eyes
of watchful
cats applaud you.

POWERLESS

I am the one
that has fallen
from the flight
in the middle of the night.

Fluttering,
    trying
            sputtering
i await to die.
am pitiful
    and grotesque
i must fight!

On and on
    the flight
        goes to greet dawn.

LA LUZ DEL DIA

A passing light
roared throughout the sky
attacking the dormant night.
Its outstretched arms
pounced on the mesquites
and on rooftops below.
The silent shadows
ran for cover
hiding from its wrath.

A SPARROW ON A WALK

A giddy sparrow
inspected the branches
on my tree.

It nervously hopped
back and forth
forth and back
looking for something
that appeared lost.

For several moments
he played this game
then suddenly he flew away
as an alley cat
wanted him as prey.

MESTIZOS

*Los mezquites
levantaron
los mestizos.*

*Llevandolos al altar del sol
rezaron por las caras morenas,
hijos del sol.*

*La luna se sonrio.
abrazando los mestizos
un beso les dio.*

SOY

Me.

I am.

I walk through
the glass corridors
of my mind
seeing reflections
of gold, red and black
pass by.

I am.

PART III

We landed on the moon but failed to capture its light.

DEATH

Death comes to all
       it creeps
        or dances
through the countless
           leaves
of the gigantic tree of
           time.

We are
   the walking dead.

HIGHWAY 44

I was driving my car
through highway 44
on a night dressed with the moon's blue skirts.
i peeked through my rear-view mirror
and saw the lights of Alice
slowly hide behind the horizon.
my car sped west in search of adventure
i merely was its passenger.

Adjusting the radio
i saw a shadow some distance away.
without thinking much more about it
i continued my journey.
another beer i easily gulped
down my gut that protested quite loudly.

Again i saw the shadow
but this time it took the shape of a man
a hitch-hiker that i considered offering a ride to.
but changed my mind as i sped past him
at eighty miles an hour.
opening my window to throw an empty beer bottle
i saw the shadow run past me
and it stopped for a split-second
in front of the car
waved good-bye, smiled and sped on.

CONTEMPLATING

It uses
its three
sometimes large
sometimes small
skinny hands
to wipe its blemished face.

With each and every wipe
it carries all
man, beast and universe
to a smaller place
leaving only
bits and pieces
of broken glass.

A SPROUTING BEAN

It reached towards the sky
with its sprawling limbs
and sighed with ecstasy
as the grass below
tickled its sides.

The giddy sparrows
giggled as they flew by
enjoying this scene.

EL PISCADOR

*Aqui en mi surco
miro los gusanos
metiendose entre los capullos
besando el algodon.*

*Aqui sentado
siento el aire
chicoteando mi cara
a que 'scurra el sudor.*

*las caras de las matas
esperan que mis manos
arranquen sus ojos blancos
hechandolos al costal.*

*Y el gato prieto
espera que caiga el sol.*

NO NAME

¿De que bola
de luz viene esa mujer
que baila en el cielo de obscuridad?

Mis manos se cubren
de llanto
cuando juega con su pecho.

Mi corazon rebienta
de calor y deseo.
pero ella nomas baila:
         brincando la luna
         y riendose del sol.

CHELLA

*Un
gusanito verde
y lleno de vello
subio el anaqua
a ver a su novia,
Chella.*

*Crusando
la ultima rama
vio a una chista
llevarse a
ella.*

*Grito
el pobre gusanito
y cayendose en el
zacate un poquito se
espino.*

*Se fue por el camino
buscando a ella,
su novia que con
la chista se
juyo.*

THE CEILING

A glass ceiling
clings between earth and space.
Only shimmering rays
of red, blue, and yellow
pierce its frozen body.

LA LAMPARITA SIN LUZ

Una mujer misteriosa
    anda por el cielo
    buscando su luz,
una luz
      para su lamparita.

Con sus pasos de gato
    she hides in the clouds
    stalking the runaway light
pero
    la luz se pasa
    through her guts.
    y se va corriendo
    bouncing *de estrella*
      a estrella.

Ella,
    se va sigüiendo
    buscando su luz.

ESPERANZA

*¿De que origin
viene esa mujer?*

She rolls her wheelbarrel
across the paths of time.

Con sus manos morenas
she scoops,
      large glittering handfuls
    of fire,
        scattering 'em
        everywhere.

Los mezquites gritan de llanto while
combing her long black hair.

*Ella se sonrie
y se va.*

JUST A TREE

I wish
that i could be
a tree
a mesquite
that lives
like it does.

But,
how can i
say such a thing
if it too
searches the heavens
with its outstretched limbs
and has nothing
but its arms.

TO VISUALIZE

A soñar sueños
is a favorite pastime
many people think of it as a
fad
and will pass with time.

Pero,
it will always be
porque sin sueños no
se hace nada.

If years back
men could not visualize
some call it fantasize
mucho o sino todo lo de 'hora
would not have materialized.

¡Que sueñen todos!
Pero con medida
porque,
como todas las cosas
mucho de hacer
se a desperdeser.

A soñar
soñar . . . y hacer.

WHO?

Purrrr . . .
        . . . rings through the ears
      of every creature
      calming their innermost fears.

Vultures,
       lions
           lambs
               and peacocks
rush to the sacred place
that's laid underneath
every stone and blade of grass.

Flying,
      walking,
           running
               and crawling

they must get
to that place!

UN HOMBRE

Pasaba por el arroyo
un hombre
swaying from side to side.

His bluish hair
pampered
his golden face
and teased
sus ojos de piedra
reflecting
light from the stars.

Un hombre grande
poderoso
walked *el arroyo*.

Pero nadie sabe
what he was
or what he wanted
nomas que el arroyo
se lo trago.

VIENDO AL CIELO

Vide al cielo
carcajearse tanto
que lloraba de gusto.
sus ojos
humedos de lagrimas
voltearon a ver a la luna
y con sus manos
un apreton le dio.

Se rien los dos,
el cielo y la luna,
con tanta fuerza
que el temblor
de las carcajadas
despertaron al mundo y al sol.

Levantandose de sus sueños
se dieron una mirada
uno al otro.
y con entendimiento secreto
se acercaron contra
los dos que se carcajeaban
y unos chingasos
les dieron.

El cielo tiro su grito
y la luna el pelo se arranco.
corrieron los dos juntos,
a esconderse
de los dos locos,
el mundo y el sol.

Ahora,
carcajeandose
se acostaron juntos,
el mundo y el sol
para hacer el amor.

UNA MUJER

*Donde la tierra
encuentra el cielo*
dances a woman
desnuda.

Juega con las estrellas
contemplates with the sun
llora cerca del mar.

She marches through the fields
bathing *con el sudor
de los piscadores.*

*Corre por la noche
a consolar un pobre borracho
que no puede sostener
su familia.*

*Una gran mujer
es esta reina*
full of courage and valor
her golden sword adorned
con las planetas de la noche
make testimony of that.

*Los mezquites
sonrien
cuando oyen su sospiro*
lifting her hair
*con sus manos
manos de la tierra.*

Her whispers
of love, hate, war,
poverty and even jealousy
become mountains
de piedra
allí corre la sangre.

She continues her eternal dance
haciendo el collar
that clings on her bare breasts
brilliant with lights and colors
a necklace made of stones
thoughts and ideas.

Si,
es una gran mujer
esta reina
madre de mi gente
hija del sol.

LOS SUEÑOS

Siento
              that many times
              we live to be things
              that we will never be
but
   how can sanity last
   if fantasy
              cannot extend
              its hands of being?

Suspendidos
              en el aire
              as the cool breeze
              tickles our naked backs
soñamos
        de mundos
        that change
        at our will.
we
   dive in oceanic waters
   to their very depths
   juntando las riquezas
              that lie on the floor
              as apathetic fish
              run in fright.

Yes
   "to be," as Shakespeare said
   in his eternal words
   is not an easy thing.

   but
      what can we do?
            but to follow the beckoning calls
            of floating seagulls
y
  resar que la lumbre del sol
  sea eterna.

Nos
  bañamos en sueños y deseos
  striving to achieve.
          the landing on the moon in '69
          was supposedly a time
          of rejoicing for all.
¿llegamos allí
y ahore que?
      on to mars, venus or mercury
      or maybe . . . maybe

Maybe war?
a darnos guerra
unos a los otros
          each wrapped up in their dreams
          of having a better place for man
          on this rotating planet.
bronze men
      march to meet
      the clanging machines
      that roar over the hills
to display
      their bravery
      for their country and God.
      all to die
and adorn
      con sus cuerpos
      the embracing arms
      of the world.

their lips
whose heart no longer beats
      eat the dirt
      below them
      never to digest it.
¿porque?

Watching
    the giddy sparrows
    play their tedious games
    on *Los Mezquites De Siempre*
    we lay down to rest.
there
    our thoughts
    gather moss
      pero nuestras aimas
      gritan de gusto
      al ver el sol.

The golden chariots
    of flying angels
    streak through
    the sky of emptiness.
sus chicotes
    break the silence
    that hides in the shadows
    of the dancing mesquites.
con sus
    caballos negros
    sigen en su marcha!

Our world
    of broken dreams
    and promises that never were
entangle
    our very soul
    move on! forward!
¿para qué?

Cities
>   with neon lights
>   and pregnant buildings

carve
>   their presence
>   *en la alma del mundo.*

flying
>   jets scream
>   their victorious roar

scoffing
>   at creatures
>   that crawl below.

yes
>   to achieve
>   and build

is
>   our quest
>   as our tentacles

search
>   the air, sea and space
>   for something more!

much
>   much more!
>   and we scribble on

our
>   note pad of centuries
>   to keep proper score.

Bendecimos
>   *nuestras casas*
>   making holy
>   our places of worship.

our
>   prophets and men of the word
>   preach through the streets

to
>   make holy our creations
>   of plastics and jets.

Sí
>*muchas veces* we live
>but never to be.

solamente
>>*un sueño* of fantasy
>>*a levantarnos otra vez*
>>*Del Mezquite De Siempre*

to
  walk
    build
and
  maybe sleep
  for eternity.

JUST WONDERING

I often wonder
what it's all about.
Our reason for being here
has been asked
a million times over
the years of our existence
Para qué es todo?
The human mind
and soul two different
things yet running in unison
debate over it!
Padre de mis padres
te ruego
que me oigas.
If there is no heaven
then at least
let there be peace of mind.

ARROYO

El arroyo awoke
to the soft soothing
rays of the sun
that stroked its exposed belly.

It yawned
and gently moved
its body to nowhere.

PAPER

Paper.
Paper! Paper!
The paper monster is here!
see there
its belly breathes
and eyes of letters typed
stare at the plastic walls.

It laughs and cries
and orders its directives
to all concerned.
Even here,
under my hand
it apathetically lays
ready to record
in written form
my inner thoughts.

Filed here
kept there
it breathes in
its life-sustaining air.

The paper monster is here
to be and live
till we no longer be.

ESPERANDO

Sentado en mi cuarto
espere que llegara
el angel de mi guardia
para decirle que era tiempo
de despedirnos.

PART IV

Closing our eyelids, we are surrounded by darkness and sleep.

DREAMING

Sueños are part of my world
'cause they make me think of you,
the way our love can be.

I dream of us
strolling through the beach
y pensando how our life is going to be.
together *con amor y compasión*.

You to be you is what i dream.
y yo to be me
but able to express the pounding i feel
when i see you look at me.
free to tell you
que my legs get weak
when i get close to you.

Pero son sueños, me dicen
and dreams are for fools.
perhaps,
but they give to me your love
that otherwise i could not have.

Son los sueños
que me dan a mi tus besos.
siento la calor de tu cuerpo
in my dreams of being me
and by being me having you
to share with only me.

MACARIO

Desperto el mundo
con una mañana fresca
that sat on the streets
of this city.

Gente walked *de cornor a cornor*
haciendo el trafico del dia.
Streets' lights apathetically
turned their red, amber and green faces
to the ever moving cars, trucks and people.

There,
on *la plaza*'s bench
across from the yellow skinny church
slept *Macario*
un viejito de muchos años.

He yawned
scratched his stubby chin
and turned on his side
and fell asleep again.
y los angeles del sol
rolled the blankets of the night
towards the horizon on the west.

Macario empezo a soñar
as *los mezquites*
dressed themselves
preparing for the day
y las chistas gossiped.

*La cocina respiraba
del aroma de frijoles refritos
que Sylvia,
la esposa de macario
cociniaba.*

*Oia su voz
que le dicia
"Macario levantate
es tiempo. tienes que ir a trabajar."
y las tortillas en el comal*
whispered tempting words
to his growling stomach.

*" 'ta bueno vieja.
dame un tragito de cafe.' "
la tasa que le traiba Sylvia
brinca de calentura.*

*Sentandose Macario
en la cama que el creia
desperto.
Pensaba, nomas es banco*
as *una lagrima gritaba.*
*Sacco su botella de mescal
y un trajo le dio.*

REFLECTIONS

Sitting here i wonder
how long my sanity will last.
how can i say to you
the things that my heart
anxiously waits to scream?

Must i succumb to nothing?
must i do what my body must
and my being repulses?
i guess i have no choice.

Must i destroy my very being
to please this . . . this thing?
my rational mind
says "no"
but my soul screams
to follow you,
you that are reflections
of shattered glass.

A FLYING THING

A flying thing
rode through the clouds
of my mind.
it swayed from side to side
playing with the water below
splashing it on my face.
my eyes red with desire
cried for it to stop.

It only giggled
and continued on its merry game
laughing . . . playing
with its new found toy.
"here i am," it shouted,
"come get me."

Angrily i reached for it
and grabbed it
by its throat
choked it and died.

AQUI Y AYA

Walking . . .
        talking . . .
                running . . .
crawling . . .
        smiling . . .
                laughing . . .
    . . . my eyes are crying.

On a cruise . . .
        flying . . .
                sailing.
i am all confused.
no voice
        only mumbling sounds
        pound within.

Smiling . . .
        laughing . . .
my falling tears
        feed every river
        and creature
giving life or death
whichever is which.

SOMBRA

*¿Por qué me sigue
esta sombra de nada?
la sombra de hacer
pero siempre vivir en sueños,
sueños de nacer.*

SOMETIMES A PROUD STAR

There
far, far from the sleeping hill
lingers a shimmering star
that hides from the naked eye.

A shy star it is
but when the nights
are covered with obnoxious clouds
it stands proud
pounding its chest.

At times
it even joins the sun
but hides behind his
glittering vest.

ENTICEMENT

The colorful glass
spun its web of delight
on table tops
as naked women
enticed wide-eyed men.
they danced!

They smiled
and gently caressed their breasts
to the wild roar of horny men.

Masturbate!
They screamed
and quickly left
center stage.

A *MEDUZA*

A *meduza* of a thousand faces
i see walking through
the corridors of this hall.
her countless eyes
changing expressions every time
i see it run through
the reflections of mirrors
that stand still
for the hands of time.

Her tentacles reach through
the depths of my secrets and dreams
she freezes them
and picks them up
as a new child that it is.
whining and crying it wiggles
as birth it has been given
by this woman of endless time and whims.

Kissing its lips
i gaze into its eyes
and freeze never to breathe
but always to be.

UN NIÑO

A small child
played by the beach.
He tossed clods
of sand to the sea.
Laughing at the wind
he groped the waves
as they bathed him
with their beckoning
call to follow them
where their mother lay.

Lazy seagulls
floated in the air
screeching their desire
for a scrap of food.
the child
looking at them
tossed up in the air
a stale piece of bread.
With ease and grace
one caught it
in midair
dashed to the sea
and fed it to the waves.

SITTING ALONE

Sentado, solo
here by the window
pienso of yesterdays
when the wind
was kind to my bones.

I think of cold nights
sharing *mis colchitas*
with my wife
next to me.
A house full
of warmth and trying times.
We laughed
We cried
We argued over big and petty things
Pero nunca
estube solo!
Ni pense que
haci iba hacer.

Now I wonder
para qué fue todo
si nomas para morir de soledad naci?
I remember my sons and daughters
running to my side
que les contara cuentitos
to pass the night away.

que bonito eran
esos tiempos
that i thought would never pass.
now they've grown and moved away
moved far . . . far away.
i yearn for someone
and here i sit alone.

Que llegara algüien ahorita
el cartero
o el lechero
para platicarles
de los tiempos pasados.

¿Ahora pienso
para qué fue todo
si nomas para morir de soledad naci?

Sitting alone
by the window
i see *el mezquite*
bowing to the earth
and is no more.

Haci sere yo.
i must turn in for the night
and greet *mis colchitas*
so they'll smile
and warm my aching bones.

¿Ahora pienso
para qué fue todo
si nomas para morir de soledad naci?

A WALKING MAN

Ese hombre
andaba de lado a lado
en un callejon
la noche pasada
chiflando su cancion.

Se pescaba
de las casas
para hacerlas entender.
pero nomas se caia
a levantarse otra vez.

Bailaba con los mezquites.
trompesandose cayo
dio su grito
y allí murio.

MEZQUITE TREE

The cold earth
        awaits
                your coming
the grass is brittle
as the stinging
        whip of the wind
tears every hair
        every strand
                to pieces.
Come, come
to the barren earth
she's sterile
        nothing moves
        only breathes.

Come and lay your cloak
of white
on every form and limb
freeze them
        purify them
don't let'em die!

Quickly, now,
we can't wait
        hurry
swiftly place your face
on the hands
        of the mezquite trees
        make 'em white!

THIS BUILDING

La luz del dia
runs through
the corridors
of this time-suspended building.

Fast-moving ants
dressed in white
try to give it life.
y resuella.

Faster,
       faster,
            faster
their feet slap the floor
below them!

The building *despierta*
muy asustado.
despues enojandose
se come las hormigas blancas.
Acabando.
eruta y se duerme.

UNOS OJOS

Miro unos ojos cafeses,
color de llanto,
los parparos
con pestañas negras
penetran mi corazon.

Miro el gato prieto
dar su sonrisa
y corre por las sombras
de mi llanto.

Tú me das
un beso con tus ojos
y te vas
sigüiendo el gato prieto.

MIDNIGHT SUN

Lifting my heart
to the midnight sun
i bowed
to its shimmering light.

¿*ELLA ES*?

*¿De qué origen
viene esa mujer?*

*She rolls her wheelbarrow
across the paths of time.*

Con sus manos morenas
she scoops large, glittering
handfuls of fire
scattering 'em everywhere.

Los mezquites gritan de llanto
while combing her jet-black hair.

*Ella se sonrie
y se va.*

¿TÚ ERES?

*Tú eres
la tierra
mojada de llanto
esperando que retoñe
el mezquite.*

*Sus ramas
secas y largas
peinan las nubes
en desesperacion.*

*¿Los pajaros locos
volan
a la vuelta y vuelta
sabiendo que la sombra de nada
te cubrara!*

*Y las nauas del sol
mueven el aire
que grita entre las ramas
con burla y compasion.*

*Torsiendose y retorsiendose
espera el mezquite.*

Esperando.

AN INTOXICATED MOON

Sitting on my doorsteps
I watched the moon peak
through the silk hair of the earth
and drink from a goblet
red sweet wine.

She licked her lips
in a very sensuous manner
giggled
and drank some more.

MI SURCO

Sentado en este surco
      miro una luz
           Brillante!
Its hot breath
      runs through my spine

Una mujer con una lampara
      da sus pasos de gato
        buscando,
           buscando algo.
Aquí sentando,
    miro el sol
      saliendo.

WRITING CAN BE

Paper and ink can be
such a freedom of expression
dreams and paradises
come to be
at will
thoughts and philosophies
take written form.

Yet
many times it can be a sickness
making us its victims
plagued with vomiting of words
words and phrases
writing for what seems
to be an eternity.

BOOK TWO

ENGLISH TRANSLATIONS

THE ROLLING BARREL

A small barrel full of air
began to roll down
the trail that cuts across
the creek.
slowly . . . slowly it rolled . . .
gathering speed as it went . . .
faster . . . faster . . . faster it ran
kissing the caliche rocks
and waving, "bye" to the quelites
and shouting, "look at me i am free!"

It glided gracefully
as it splashed
in the muddy water of the creek.
there it enthusiastically swayed from side to side
bathing itself as it floated down the creek
till somewhat tired it came to a halt
on the banks of this majestic place.
it ran no further.

Some tiny growing hands
baked by the rays of the moon and sun
picked it up again.
its belly full of water
screamed of joy
as it again began to roll down the hill
as before.

now at even a faster pace
it flew down.
because of its great speed
it could no longer kiss the stones.
the quelites and mesquite trees
embracing each other
laughed and crawled
on the soil below.

Jumping and bouncing
it rolled down ever-so-fast.
desperately it tried to grab
the hands of the clouds
that watched it without concern.

Till finally,
the moaning sounds of *la llorona*
stabbed every creature to silence
as the creek slowly swallowed it.
down in the very depths of the creek
it is buried
never to be seen again.

NACER

Why does this shadow,
shadow of nothingness
follow me?
The shadow of doing
but always to live in dreams,
dreams to be born again.

DROPLETS

The tears of crying souls
are flowing
       in the body of earth
in lakes,
    rivers
        and falls as droplets
        of diamonds
to awaiting hands.

The eyes and lips
of the king of apes
give a sparkle and speak of terms.
a sparkling light
       that has glimmered
since the birth of time
set to invite,
    as guests,
       its prey.
then to become knives and swords
with a coat of blood and torn flesh.
and the screaming sounds
       of battling winds
       fill the air.

The crowned king
of colored lights,
       plastics and jets
gives his words
of promises and love.

lips of firmness
        and tenderness
assure the spoken words
with laws from heaven.
yet the sharp teeth
        sink into warm flesh
making the blood spurt
        and smear his face.
and the screaming sounds
of battling winds
fill the air.

The tears of crying souls
are flowing in the body of earth
in lakes, rivers and fall as droplets
        of diamonds.

COSAS **OF THE WORLD**

Some hands emerge from the human form
showing the traces of their veins
they scratch
        the earth
making holes
that fill with vomit
        and the poor earth
        responds
            with shrieking sounds
            of lost souls
piercing the heart of silence.

A menace
these crying sounds
        soil the bedspreads
        of the human race
it turns the golden thrones and crowns
        to a mossy green
        filthy and rotten.

And the crying sound continues
        it follows the wind
        falls with the rain
the branches
of everything
      hold
        the captive souls.

The chieftains
of every tribe
      begin their dance
      they fan the spirits
      with their golden feathers
their chanting voices
and their splashing feet
      smear the people
      bathe!
      and participate!
Lakes of vomit are born
here the people bathe
      full of joy
      and laughter
the nails of the gnawing hands
        become red
        with filth
only
    the groaning sounds
    of struggling winds
        can be heard
        by certain ears.

RAYOS OF THE SUN

The sun's rays
accompanied by the wind
brush every blade of grass
that stands or bows.
people with multiple-faces
   laugh and go throughout the world
making codes and proclamations
      thanking God for life.
the clouds in the sky
release their anguish
      on every plant and person.
a furious wind roars
through the trees
shouting in the ears of every person:
      "Look at me! And Beware!"

Encircled with lights
of every conceivable color
people watch to see
      their mold take form,
used to their bidding.

From the dirt
    a mumbled shriek
filters through the surface
exhausted
and bearing the stomping feet
of the festival above.

no one listens
only laughter rumbles
so very hard that
    the oceans and mountains
    tremble.
the birds and flowers
    spin, spin and fall.
lightning, of vengeance,
red with fire
    points at everything
to suck the blood
    of every walking creature.

The light of the human race
is gone.
    they're running in darkness
    others cry out, as they crawl:
      "I. I."

Everything pukes
    their excess water
until nothing stands
only the vomit
    color of death.

Calmness returns
    to the skies.
and the world
silently
begins to breathe.
from the dirt
    come
    the frogs
    the new kings.

LA LECHUSA

On a clear night
i sat on my front porch
to await what the night would bring.

I remember it so well
because what I am about to say
is hard to believe
but true.

Flying close to the moon
screamed a white owl
that many people believed was a witch.
it said things that my ears
couldn't comprehend
but my soul trembled in fear.
the face of the moon
blushed in an orange tint.
i wondered what it was
that this creature
spouted to me . . . or to the earth?

I reached high to the sky
and grabbed the moon's passing light
and held it close to my chest
hoping that that thing
would leave and never return.

The cool hands of the wind
slapped me back . . . it's just an owl.
. . . nothing to worry about . . .
it's not logical.
feeling more at ease i petted my little dog
that sat right beside me.
i grabbed her
flapped my wings
and flew towards the moon to turn in for the night.

YO

I am the masked man
that penetrates
every feeling and every pulse.
i see everything with my single eye
that's large and green.
i am in every man waiting to be free.
i board every ship, car and train.

Yes, i've traveled through
the canals of time and space.
i'm here and there
waiting to show myself
and proclaim my very being!

But it's impossible
'cause you might . . . harm me . . . or kill me.
kill me?
impossible! 'cause i cannot die.

GRITO

When i heard a shriek
run through the branches
of the trees,
the moon awoke.

The dogs barked
or sang?
i really . . . don't remember.

LAS NUBES

I laid
on my sack that i used for picking cotton.
as i stared at the sky
the clouds lifted
their skirts
and fled.

I begged them
to return
so that i could embrace them
and for them to irrigate my heart.

If they did this
i would feel my soul
renewed and free
from this black cat
that sleeps on my chest.

GUSANITO

I am overjoyed
when i see the dove
fly from the sun.

Fluttering its wings
it rests in its nest
to sing its song.

The little worm emerges,
squirming out of its hole
hitting himself on his chest
he screams, "fly back to the sun!"

As the black cat arrives
the little dove no longer sings
and flies back following the shadows of the sun.

And the little worm
goes back to its hole
to eat his bowl of beans.

¿QUÉ SEÑORA?

It was a foggy morning when
an old woman dressed in black
prowled the streets of San Diego
her flour-colored hair
danced in the wind.
the dogs barked
and the cats hid out of sight.

Arriving on the corner
of Mier and Highway 44
she stopped.
there
with her raisin eyes
she inspected the area.
she sat down.

Opening her blue purse
she pulled out
a letter yellowed with years
and the mesquite trees began to cry.
the cats came out of hiding
to converse with her
that read her letter attentively.

The purple eagle
circled near by
searching for its shadow.

when it saw the old lady
it was stricken with disease.
it fell from the sky and died.

Standing up,
she wiped her hands
and walked towards to the spot
where the eagle had fallen.
with great care
she put the eagle and the letter
in her purse.
when the sun cried bitterly
she disappeared from the earth.

A PONER

A red-feathered
old rooster
dominated his chicken house.
He always went to bed
with the cream of the crop.
he didn't care
if they were dark, white,
red or whatever color of plumage.
anyway they
all laid eggs.

THE FOREST

From the fertile earth
a human plant emerges.
with its arms clasped
together pointing towards the sky,
they stretch out
to caress the rays of the sun,
brown hands
that play with the wind
swaying from side to side.

The barren fields become forests
as they multiply
dancing with the light of the moon
and the stars.

Blooms of murky white
decorate the blue walls
of the heavens
as red stripes
run through their fields
catching every seed
making them sterile.
They live
and breathe
because their years are numbered
when they'll return
to the earth,
and be no more!

A SEMBRAR

Picking the words
of my past
i sat down
between the furrows
to count them.

A book
of these words and phrases
i was to make
praying that they would grow wings
so that they would
fly through the fields
and in time
become a new breed
in the planting season.

ROSES

The rose bush dressed itself in its green suit
to wait for the man
the man that gave it gifts of jewelry,
jewelry made of rubies.

Its eyes brilliant of want
and desperation,
"oh . . . when will he come?"
it asked the bee
that flew close by.
"woman, i don't know . . . but i hope it's soon
because i also want to see your rings, necklaces and pins.
i know they'll be beautiful . . . i wait to touch 'em
so that the evil eye will not befall 'em."

When the man arrived
the tree
who was the neighbor of the rose bush
exclaimed, "look! the man has arrived!
look the rose bush it has its gift!
they're brilliant jewels!"
"how strange . . . " said the bee
"they're not rubies but gold."
and the bush sighed
and expelled its breath
and died.

MI SEÑORA

My lady is a woman
dressed with the desire to serve
her sons, grandchildren and cousins.
with her brown hands
she gives them a bath and combs their hair.

I remember,
that on the twenty-fourth of December
she gave her human gift
to her kin.
overjoyed several bathed
in the river of nothingness
but full of stars, moon and sun.

Now,
i've heard it said that my lady
visits her kin and with a kiss
she says, "embrace the fire of the sun
as the king of kings
who is my son
is about to come!"

MESTIZOS

The mesquites
in offering
lifted the mestizos.

Taking 'em to the altar of the sun
they prayed for the brown faces
sons of the sun.

The moon smiled.
embracing and cuddling 'em
she gave them a kiss.

EL PISCADOR

Here in my furrow
i see the worms
enter the cotton-fruit
and kiss their inexperienced lips.

Sitting here
i feel the wind
whipping my face
to extract my sweat.

The faces of the cotton plants
patiently wait
for my hands to pull out
their white eyes
stuffing 'em in the sack.

And the black cat
awaits for the sun to sleep.

NO NAME

From what
mass of light
does that woman
who dances in the sky of vagueness come?

My hands
are covered with desire
when i play
with her bosom.

My heart bursts
with heat and desire.
but she only dances:

        she jumps the moon
        and laughs at the sun.

CHELLA

A
green worm
covered with fuzz
climbed the anaqua tree
to visit his sweetheart,
Chella.

While crossing
the last branch
he saw that she
was stolen by a sparrow.

He screamed
and falling below
the stickers attacked
his body.

He quietly left.
But he searched
the streets
looking for her,
Chella,
who had just
eloped with a sparrow.

LA LAMPARITA SIN LUZ

A mysterious woman
    searches the heavens
    for her light,
a light
      for her lamp.

With her cat-walk
    she hides in the clouds
    stalking the runaway light
but
    the light runs
    through her guts
    and frantically runs
    bouncing from star
        to star.

She
    leaves,
    and continues her search.

ESPERANZA

Where did
that woman originate?

She rolls her wheelbarrel
across the paths of time.

With her brown hands
she scoops,
    large glittering handfuls
    of fire,
        scattering 'em
        everywhere.

The mesquites scream with desire while
combing her long black hair.

She smiles
and leaves.

TO VISUALIZE

To dream dreams
is a favorite pastime.
many people think of it as a
fad
and will pass with time.

But,
it will always be
because without dreams
nothing can be.

If years back
men could not visualize
some call it fantasize
much or all of today
would not have materialized.

Let everyone dream!
but not to an extreme
because,
like everything else
too much of anything
will do more harm than good.

Dream
        dream . . . and create.

UN HOMBRE

A man
walked through the creek
swaying from side to side.

His bluish hair
pampered
his golden face
and teased
his eyes of rock
reflecting
light from the stars.

A huge
powerful man
walked through the creek.

But no one knows
what he was
or what he wanted,
just that the creek
had swallowed him.

VIENDO AL CIELO

I saw the sky
laugh so hard
that it cried of joy.
its eyes,
humid with tears
turned to stare at the moon
and with its hands
it embraced her.

They both laughed,
the sky and the moon,
with such force
that their laughter
awoke the earth and sun.

They lifted themselves
from their dreams
and looked at each other
with a secret understanding.
they moved towards
those that continued to laugh
and beat the fuck out of 'em.

The sky shrieked in terror
and the moon pulled out
its hair.
they ran in fright
to hide
from the mad
earth and sun.

Now
laughing
they went to bed
the earth and sun
and made love
to one another.

UNA MUJER

Where the earth
meets the sky
dances a woman
naked.

She plays with the stars
contemplates with the sun
and cries with the sea.

She marches through the fields
bathing with the sweat
of field workers.

She runs through the night
to console a poor drunk
who can't support
his family.

A great woman
is this Queen
full of courage and valor.
her golden sword adorned
with the planets of the night
make testimony of that.

The mesquites
smile
when they hear her breath
lifting her hair
with their hands
hands of the earth.

Her whispers
of love, hate, war,
poverty and even jealousy
become mountains
of solid rock
there . . . there flows blood.

She continues her eternal dance
making her necklace
that clings on her bare breasts
brilliant with lights and colors
a necklace made of stones
thoughts and ideas.

Yes,
she's a great woman
this Empress,
mother of my people
daughter of the sun.

LOS SUEÑOS

I feel
        that many times
        we live to be things
        that we will never be
but
  how can sanity last
  if fantasy
        cannot extend
        its hands of being?

Suspended
        in mid air
        as the cool breeze
        tickles our naked backs
we dream
    of worlds
    that change
    at our will.
we
  dive in oceanic waters
  to their very depths
  gathering the riches
        that lie on the floor
        as apathetic fish
        run in fright.

Yes,
  "to be," as Shakespeare said
  in his eternal words
  is not an easy thing.

but
    what can we do?
            but to follow the beckoning calls
            of floating seagulls
and
    pray that the fire of the sun
    be eternal.

We
    bathe in dreams and desires
    striving to achieve.
            the landing on the moon in '69
            was supposedly a time
            of rejoicing for all.
we got there
and now what next?
            on to mars, venus or mercury
            or may . . . maybe.

Maybe war?
to war
against each other
            each wrapped up in their dreams
            of having a better place for man
            on this rotating planet.

bronze men
        march to meet
        the clanging machines
        that roar over the hills
to display
        their bravery
        for their country and God.
        all to die
and adorn
        with their bodies

                    the embracing arms
                    of the world.
their lips
whose heart no longer beats
                    eat the dirt
                    below them
                    never to digest it.
why?

Watching
          the giddy sparrows
          play their tedious games
          on the Eternal Mesquites
          we lay down to rest.
there
          our thoughts
          gather moss
                    but our souls
                    scream with joy
                    as they see the sun.

The golden chariots
          of flying angels
          streak through
          the sky of emptiness.
their whips
          break the silence
          that hides in the shadows
          of the dancing mesquites.
with their
          black hair
          they continue their march!

Our world
          of broken dreams
          and promises that never were

entangle
> our very soul
> move on! forward!

what for?

Cities
> with neon lights
> and pregnant buildings

carve
> their presence
> on the soul of the world.

flying
> jets scream
> their victorious roar

scoffing
> at creatures
> that crawl below.

yes
  to achieve
  and build

is
 our quest
 as our tentacles

search
> the air, sea and space
> for something more!

much
   much more!
   and we scribble on

our
 note pad of centuries
 to keep proper score.

We bless
> our homes
> making holy
> our places of worship.

our
>   prophets and men of the word
>   preach through the streets
to
  make holy our creations
  of plastics and jets.

Yes,
>   many times we live
>   but never to be.
only
>   a dream of fantasy
>   to get up again from
>   the Eternal Mesquites
to
  walk
    build
and
  maybe sleep
  for eternity.

ESPERANDO

> Sitting on my furrow
> i waited for
> my guardian angel
> to tell him that
> it was time
> to bid our farewell.

MACARIO

The world awoke
to a freshly-bathed morning
that sat on the street
of this city.

People walked from corner to corner
contributing to the traffic of the day.
Streets lights apathetically
turned their red, amber and green faces
to the ever moving cars, trucks and people

There,
on a park bench
across from the yellow skinny church
slept Macario
a man of many years.

He yawned
scratched his stubby chin
and turned on his side
and fell asleep again.
and the angels of the sun
rolled the blankets of the night
towards the horizon on the west.

Macario began to dream
as the mesquites
dressed themselves
preparing for the day
and the sparrows gossiped.

The kitchen breathed
with the aroma of refried beans

that Sylvia,
Macario's wife,
cooked attentively.

He heard her call,
"Macario get up.
it's time to go to work."
and the tortillas on the skillet
whispered tempting words
to his growling stomach.

"OK, honey.
please pour me some coffee."
Sylvia brought him
a cup that jumped with heat
and vitality.

Sitting up on the bed
he thought was there
he awoke.
He thought, it's only a park bench
and a tear cried in sorrow.
he opened his bottle of Mescal
and took a gulp.

SOMBRA

Why does this shadow
of nothingness
follow me?
the shadow to build
but always to live in dreams,
dreams to be born again.

SITTING ALONE

Sitting alone,
here by the window
i think of yesterdays
when the wind
was kind to my bones.

I think of cold nights
sharing my quilts
with my wife
next to me
A house full
of warmth and trying times.
We laughed
we cried
we argued over big and petty things
but never
was i alone
and never did i think
this was to be.

Now I wonder
what was the purpose of everything
if i was born only to die of loneliness?

I remember my sons and daughters
running to my side
to tell 'em stories
to pass the night away.

how beautiful
it was then,
the times
that i thought would never pass.
now they've grown and moved away
moved far . . . far away.
i yearn for someone
and here i sit alone.

I wish someone would come,
the mailman
or milkman
to tell 'em
stories of the good ole days.

Now i wonder
what was the purpose of everything
if i was born only to die of loneliness?

Sitting alone
by the window
i see the mesquite
bowing to the earth
and is no more.

That's how i must be,
i must turn in for the night
and greet my quilts
so they'll smile
and warm my aching bones.

Now i wonder
what was the purpose
if i was born only to die of loneliness?

A WALKING MAN

A night ago
that man over there
walked in a dark alley
swaying from side to side
as he whistled his merry song.

He balanced himself
on apathetic houses
trying to make 'em understand.
but he only fell
and stood up again and again.

He danced with mesquites
stumbling again he fell
he cried out
and died.

THIS BUILDING

The light of day
runs through
the corridors
of this time-suspended building.

Fast-moving ants
dressed in white
try to give it life
and it breathes.

Faster,
       faster,
             faster
their feet slap the floor
below them!

Frightened the building
awakens.
then getting angry
he eats the white ants.

Finishing
his feast
he burps
and goes to sleep again.

UNOS OJOS

I see
a pair of brown eyes
full of want.
its lashes
brown and luscious
penetrate my heart.

I see the black cat
smile
and run through the shadows
of my desire.

You give me a kiss
with your brown eyes
and leave
following the black cat.

¿*ELLA ES?*

From what
did this woman originate?

She rolls her wheelbarrow
across the paths of time.

With her brown hands
she scoops large, glittering
handfuls of fire
scattering 'em everywhere.

The mesquites scream with want
while combing her jet black hair.

She only smiles
and quietly leaves.

¿TÚ ERES?

You are
the humid
soil of want
waiting for
the mesquite to grow.

Its branches
dry and long
comb the clouds
in anxiety.

The crazy birds
fly
circling and circling
knowing the shadow of nothingness
will cover you.

And the skirts of the sun
move the wind
that screams through the branches
with its vicious laughter.

Squirming and turning
the mesquite awaits.

and waits.

MI SURCO

Sitting on my furrow
      i see
            a brilliant light!
Its hot breath
     runs through my spine.

A woman with a lamp
     searches for something
     searches,
         and searches.
Here sitting
     i see the sun
     emerge.